PETS

getting them, caring for them, and loving them

by Mel Hammond

illustrated by Maike Plenzke

★ American Girl®

Published by American Girl Publishing

No part of this book may be used or reproduced in any manner whatsoever without written permission except in the case of brief quotations embodied in critical articles and reviews.

20 21 22 23 24 25 26 QP 10 9 8 7 6 5 4 3 2 1

Editorial Development: Mel Hammond, Barbara Stretchberry
Art Direction & Design: Jessica Rogers
Production: Caryl Boyer, Cynthia Stiles, Heather Tubwon
Illustrations: Maike Plenzke
Special thanks: Moy Ahmad, DVM; Sandra Sawchuk, DVM; Wendy Bell

Cataloging-in-Publication Data available from the Library of Congress.

americangirl.com/service

Dear Reader,

Pets fill life with laughter and love. Maybe you want a pet, but you're still trying to convince your family that you're ready. Or maybe your family already has a pet, and you want to take on more responsibilities for its care.

In this book, you'll find everything you need to know about getting a pet and giving it the best home possible. You can take quizzes, make crafts and recipes, and read advice and stories from animal-loving girls like you.

The love between a girl and her pet is one of the most special kinds of love out there. Through good times and tough times, our pets are there for us. This book will help you be there for your pet, too.

Your friends at American Girl

CONTENTS

GETTING A PET

Pets . . .

Bring joy to
everyday
moments

Teach us
to care for
others

Love us

Comfort us when we're sad or lonely

Become our best friends

Help us

TRUE
Pet Stories

Mae Li and Sadie
Age 13, Alabama

We brought Sadie home because she was the sweetest and gentlest dog at the animal shelter. She's really smart, too! When we're sick, she can tell, and she sits right next to us to make us feel better.

We show Sadie how much we love her by feeding her, petting her, and walking her—even when it's freezing outside.

Tirath and Ladypants
Age 13, California

My cat Ladypants is funny, cute, and kind. My stepdad got her before he met my mom. He tried out a lot of names, and in the end, Ladypants was the only one that fit.

She's naughty sometimes! Once she scratched the couch so much that we had to tape it back together!

Macey and Wembley
Age 13, Tennessee

Wembley's favorite spot in our house is under the table. He's always looking for food! One time, he even dumped the trash can over when we weren't home and ate all the paper towels.

Wembley is really smart. One day, I was walking him and listening to music, and I didn't see a car coming until it was almost too late. Wembley started barking and steering me in the other direction. He saved me!

Becca and Scruffy
Age 12, New Jersey

Some people call you *scruffy* if you have a bit of a beard. Since my pet is a bearded dragon, I thought Scruffy (short for Scruffa-luffagus) would be the perfect name!

Scruffy loves to climb up high, anywhere in the house. She likes to be on top of the world! And if she gets lost, she knows how to make noise so we can find her.

Tilly and Nutmeg
Age 11, Florida

Nutmeg is a chubby, squeaky, food-loving guinea pig. We named her Nutmeg because she's brown, like the spice.

Nutmeg can be a little feisty sometimes, and she makes us laugh! One time, I left her at a friend's house and she climbed into a bin of hay. Another time, we put her on the piano and she moved around to make music.

Are You Ready for a Pet?

Hold on! Don't run to the animal shelter yet. Caring for a pet is *a lot* of work. Are you ready?

1. It's snowing outside, but your dog Jellybeans is wagging her tail at the door like she needs to go out. You . . .

    a. ask your dad to take her out. You're busy making hot chocolate, and it's freezing out there!

    b. suck it up. You throw on your coat and grab the leash.

    c. pretend to be napping. Someone else will take Jellybeans out when she starts whining.

2. How messy is your room?

    a. You clean up when your parents ask you to or when someone is coming to visit.

    b. Your floor is usually pretty clean, and you like to keep your things tidy.

    c. You have to bulldoze a path to get to your bed.

3. You're cat-sitting for your Aunt Octavia while she's out of town, and the cat throws up all over your couch. You . . .

   a. tell your mom and ask her what to do.

   b. clean up the mess. Then you keep an eye on the cat to make sure he doesn't act sluggish, lose his appetite, or vomit again. If he seems sick, you call your aunt or the veterinarian.

   c. carry the cat into another room to watch a movie together. It's too stinky to stay on the couch with all that barf!

4. You beg your parents to take a stargazing class because you're *obsessed* with outer space. But the first session isn't what you thought it would be—there are lots of boring worksheets to fill out for homework. You . . .

   a. ask your parents to help you finish the worksheets.

   b. do the worksheets and ask the teacher for some fun stargazing activities you can do on your own.

   c. quit the class and join cooking club instead. You don't like stars *that* much.

5. Your family is going to New Mexico for a week, so you won't be able to water the backyard garden you're in charge of. You . . .

   a. see if your mom has installed that automatic sprinkler system yet.

   b. ask your neighbors if they can care for the garden while you're gone. You write clear instructions and leave a phone number where they can reach you. You'll bring back a souvenir to say thank you!

   c. do nothing. It will probably rain anyway.

6. Your best friend asks you to take care of her snake, William Snakespeare, for two weeks. He eats frozen mice. You . . .

a. agree to take care of him but ask your mom to do the feedings.

b. practice feeding him with your friend to make sure you can do it correctly. If you're too squeamish to touch the mouse, you apologize to your friend and explain that you aren't the right person to care for William.

c. agree to take care of him, but just feed him hot dogs instead. There's no *way* you're bringing frozen mice into your house.

7. It's a week before your birthday party at the trampoline park, and your rabbit Cinnamon Bun has an infected tooth. The veterinarian says she needs a dental procedure. You . . .

a. rake leaves in your neighborhood to help pay for the procedure.

b. ask your parents for a birthday party at home so they can put money toward Cinnamon Bun's procedure instead. You'll also use some of the money you've saved for emergencies like this.

c. don't worry too much about it. Your parents will take care of it.

8. You get home to find that your cockatiel Belinda has escaped her cage and pooped all over your brother's latest sewing project. You . . .

a. wait for your brother to get home so you can clean up the mess together.

b. get out your gloves, spray bottle, and sponge to clean up the mess. When your brother gets home, you apologize and promise to keep Belinda in her cage from now on.

c. call your friend and ask if she wants a pet bird. You can't take this constant pooping anymore.

9. You love corgis more than anything else in the world—and your animal shelter has one available! But when you read a book about corgis, you find out that they require more walks and training than other breeds, and you were just about to join a traveling soccer team. You . . .

a. adopt a senior cat instead. The shelter volunteer says the cat likes to be lazy, so she won't mind if you're a little busy with soccer right now.

b. put soccer on hold and sign up for agility training with your newly adopted corgi.

c. adopt the corgi anyway. That book must be exaggerating. How could anything this cute be that much work?

Answers

Mostly a's

You're not ready to take care of an animal by yourself, but you'd be a great helper. If your family is ready for a pet, let your parents know what tasks you'd like to help with. Start with small duties, such as putting food in the dog's bowl or vacuuming cat fur from the couch. Slowly, you'll improve your pet care skills. One day, you might be ready to get a pet of your own!

Mostly b's

You make pet care look easy! You have a good idea of how to keep an animal happy, healthy, and safe. If your parents say it's OK, you might be ready for a pet of your own. Remember, though, that even responsible pet owners need help sometimes. Don't be afraid to ask for it! And even if your parents say no to a pet right now, you'd do a great job pet-sitting for friends and neighbors!

Mostly c's

Put on the brakes—you're not quite ready for a pet. You might love watching videos of puppies splashing in the bathtub, but feeding, grooming, and exercising an animal every day is a different story. Work on showing that you're responsible by finishing your homework, cleaning up after yourself, and finishing projects that you start. Soon, you may be ready to help care for a family pet.

Persuading Your Parents

So, you think you're ready for an animal to join the family. How do you get your parents on board?

Show that you're responsible

Do chores without being reminded, finish your homework early, and be a good role model for younger family members.

Take care of other people's pets

With a parent's permission, volunteer to walk dogs or pet-sit in your neighborhood. If your friend has a pet, ask if you can help out with feeding, cleaning, and exercising.

Volunteer

Animal shelters are great places to help care for cats, dogs, rabbits, and other animals. Ask a parent to help you research volunteer opportunities for kids. Even if you're not old enough to care for the animals, you can show your dedication by helping with adoption drives or fundraisers. Find more volunteer ideas on page 84.

PET CARE PLAN

DAILY
- 2 CUPS DRY FOOD
- 2 WALKS
- 30 MINUTES PLAYTIME
- BRUSH FUR
- REFILL WATER BOWL

WEEKLY
- BRUSH TEETH 3X
- WASH BED

Create a pet care plan

Make a list of everything your pet would need. How much food would it eat? How often would you give it exercise? Who would take care of it if your family goes on vacation? Showing that you've thought through these questions will let your parents know how serious you are about getting a pet.

Animal Advice

I really, really want a cat. All I have right now is a rabbit. I love my rabbit, but I still want a cat. My parents won't even let me volunteer with cats at an animal shelter. Do they think I'm not responsible enough?
Eliza

Your parents might be worried about the extra time, food, and supplies a cat would need. Plus, a cat might not get along with your rabbit. For now, be the best rabbit owner you can be. If your parents see how well you take care of your bunny without being reminded, they might be more willing to consider a second pet.

I think a pet would be a great companion for me. We have a lot of tough things going on at home, and I could use a pet that would always be there for me. We rent our apartment, though, and my mom gets stressed out when I ask.
Ariana

Most apartments have rules about what kinds of pets are allowed, and some don't allow pets at all. If your mom has already said no, that's final. But if she's still considering adding a pet to the family, try suggesting a low-stress pet, like a fish. A fish can provide a friendly face every day without being too expensive or hard to care for.

I want a horse, but my mom says it's a really big responsibility. How can I show her that I *am* responsible?

Amina

Caring for a horse can take several hours every day. Plus, horses are very expensive. If your heart's set on having one of your own, ask your mom if you can volunteer at a barn or attend a horse camp. If you show excitement for tasks like hauling water and shoveling manure, she might start to understand how much getting a horse means to you. You might also decide that you can have fun riding and grooming a horse without owning it yourself!

Animals are my life. The problem is, I'm allergic to cats and dogs, which are two of my top five favorite animals. I don't want a shot or anything. I just want my allergies to go away! What should I do?

Iris

Allergies are so frustrating! Some cats and dogs are hypoallergenic, which means they don't tend to aggravate people's allergies. Try meeting a cat or dog like this to see how your body reacts. Also, consider an animal without fur, such as a fish or snake. They might not be as cuddly as cats and dogs, but they can still be a lot of fun to play with—without making you wheezy and miserable.

Paying for a Pet

The feeling of a new puppy licking your face is priceless—but that puppy's food, equipment, and vet bills are not. Depending on the type of animal, your family might need to pay for . . .

Adoption fees or breeder costs

Spaying or neutering

Prevention for worms, fleas, and ticks

Microchipping and registration

Vaccinations

Equipment and supplies (see page 33 for more on that)

Food

Pet sitting, for when you go out of town

Training

Cleaning supplies for messes in the house

Apartment fees, if your family rents

Yearly vet check-ups

Grooming

Emergency vet visits, if your pet gets sick or hurt

Pet insurance

Decide with your family who will pay for what. Will your parents cover the adoption fee if you pay for food and toys? How will you earn the money? Planning for pet costs will help prove that you're ready for the responsibility.

What Pet Is Right for You?

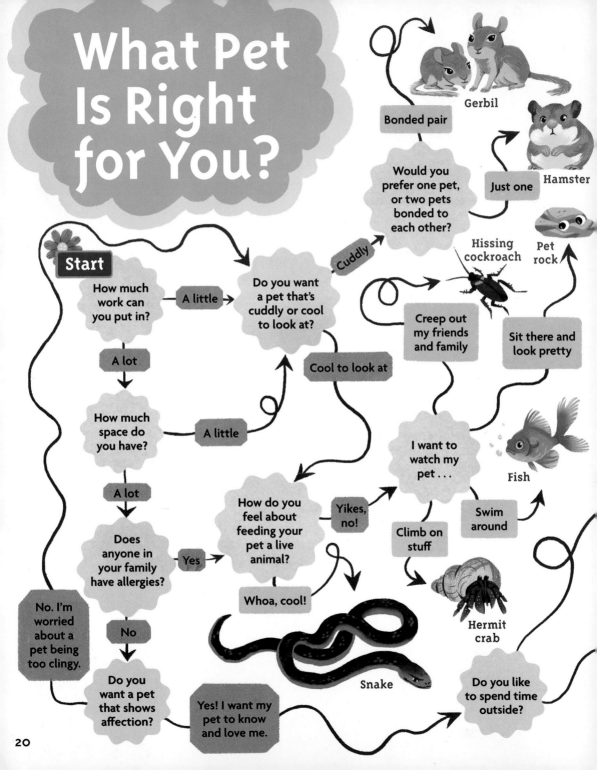

Start

How much work can you put in?
- A little →
- A lot ↓

A little → Do you want a pet that's cuddly or cool to look at?
- Cuddly →
- Cool to look at

A lot → How much space do you have?
- A little → (back to "Do you want a pet that's cuddly or cool to look at?")
- A lot ↓

Does anyone in your family have allergies?
- Yes → How do you feel about feeding your pet a live animal?
- No ↓

How do you feel about feeding your pet a live animal?
- Yikes, no! → I want to watch my pet . . .
- Whoa, cool! → **Snake**

I want to watch my pet . . .
- Climb on stuff → **Hermit crab**
- Swim around → **Fish**

No. I'm worried about a pet being too clingy. → (to bottom)

Do you want a pet that shows affection?
- Yes! I want my pet to know and love me. → Do you like to spend time outside?

Would you prefer one pet, or two pets bonded to each other?
- Bonded pair → **Gerbil**
- Just one → **Hamster**

Cool to look at →
- Creep out my friends and family → **Hissing cockroach**
- Sit there and look pretty → **Pet rock**

Gerbil

Hamster

Hissing cockroach

Pet rock

Fish

Hermit crab

Snake

Do you like to spend time outside?

Cat

Rat

2 to 3 years

Bunny

6 to 10 years

Bird

I'd like to put my pet in a comfy cage when I'm busy with something else.

How many years can you commit to a pet?

Cuddling

Training

Yes, I want my pet to be independent.

Do you want your pet to roam the house?

Would you rather spend time cuddling or teaching your pet tricks?

I like my quiet time!

Guinea pig

How do you feel about a loud, chatty pet?

The louder, the better!

No

Do you want a pet that can fit in your lap?

No, I'd like a big pet.

Is it OK if the pet turns your backyard into a mud pit?

Um . . . no.

Yes

Fine! Whatever is best for the pet.

Big or medium dog

Yes, I feel most comfortable around small pets.

Small dog

Pig

21

Dog Breeds

Just because you love videos of Siberian husky puppies riding robotic vacuums doesn't mean that type of dog is right for your family. All dogs deserve homes where they can get the care they need. And some dogs require a lot more care than others.

If your family has decided to get a dog, talk about what breed—or mix of breeds—might be a good fit. Of course, animal shelters often can't be sure of a dog's heritage. And even if you do know the breed mix, each dog has its own unique personality. That's why you should always meet a dog before bringing it home.

Here are just a few types of dog breeds your family might think about:

Working breeds are smart, and they learn tricks quickly. Traditionally, people raised these dogs to do tasks like pulling sleds and herding sheep. That means dogs of this type are very energetic and need lots of exercise.

Border Collie   Australian Cattle Dog   Siberian Husky

Giant breeds tend to be gentle and calm as adults, and their big size often gives their families a sense of protection. Huge dogs eat huge dinners, so be ready for expensive food bills, plus higher-than-average veterinary costs.

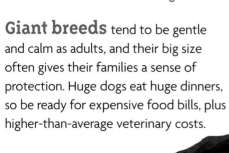

Great Dane   Irish Wolfhound   Mastiff

Non-shedding breeds

don't leave much fur around the house, so they can be a good fit for people with allergies. These dogs often require professional grooming to stay healthy, though, which can be expensive.

Goldendoodle   Poodle   Bichon Frise

Pug   Chihuahua   Pomeranian

Small breeds

don't need as much exercise as big dogs, and they can be happy in a home without a lot of space. If a small dog joins your family, expect barking, and be ready to provide plenty of dental cleanings.

Sporting breeds

love to cuddle and want to spend as much time with their families as possible. Dogs of this type, especially golden retrievers, can make excellent service animals because they're smart, easy to train, and devoted to their humans. Just make sure to give them plenty of exercise!

Labrador Retriever   Irish Setter   Golden Retriever

TRUE Pet Story
Zoe and Mochi

Thirteen-year-old Zoe B. lives with her dog Mochi, a goldendoodle. Zoe was born without arms, and Mochi helps her out with daily tasks, such as picking things up off the floor, opening doors, and finding her mom or dad when Zoe needs extra help.

Mochi isn't technically a pet—she's a working dog called a service animal. Service animals go through *a lot* of special training (usually at least 120 hours) to learn how to help someone with a disability. Until she turned eleven, Zoe did everything herself or asked someone for help when she needed it. Now that she has a service dog, life is a little easier (and cuddlier!).

"When Mochi is wearing her service vest, she knows it's time to work, and she gets very calm and focused," Zoe says. "When she's working, no one is supposed to pet her. That's so she doesn't get distracted from helping me. But at home when she's not wearing her vest, she loves to play fetch and chew on toys."

Mochi rides the school bus with Zoe and goes to all her classes. She sits under Zoe's desk and can help with tasks such as carrying papers to the front of the class. Zoe takes Mochi outside at lunchtime and lets her have a drink and go to the bathroom when she needs to.

"It's fun to have her with me," Zoe says. "I never knew a dog could be so smart and helpful. I think Mochi is the best dog in the world!" ♥

One Big, Happy Family

Bringing home a pet means adding a new member to your family. That means everyone needs to be on board. Hold a family meeting to discuss how life will change with a new pet and which tasks each person will be in charge of.

I'll take our dog on walks in the morning before school. Can someone else handle afternoon walks while I'm at softball?

I can brush our dog on weeknights, but I'll need someone else to do it when I spend weekends with my mom.

I want to feed the dog, but I might need help remembering.

Family Pet Contract

Write down each person's tasks in a contract and have everyone sign it.
Post the contract in a central location, like on the fridge or bathroom mirror.

Family Pet Contract

As the family of _____, we promise to do our best to
(pet's name)

keep our pet happy, healthy, and safe. Here are our responsibilities:

_____ will feed our pet every day and keep the water fresh.
(name)

_____ will keep our pet well groomed and clean.
(name)

_____ will give our pet exercise every day.
(name)

_____ will help train our pet so it behaves well.
(name)

_____ will play with and cuddle our pet daily.
(name)

_____ will give our pet its medicine every night.
(name)

_____

_____

Signature _____ Date _____

Signature _____ Date _____

Signature _____ Date _____

Signature _____ Date _____

Where to Get a Pet

Your family is finally ready for a pet. Where should you get one?

Animal shelters and rescues

Adopting a pet in need is the best way to help animals. Animal shelters and rescues take care of pets that are homeless, neglected, abused, or lost. They work hard to find good families who can adopt the animals and provide a safe home.

Do an internet search with your parents to see what animals are available in your area. You can find all kinds of animals that need families, from cats and dogs to mice and fish to rabbits, pigs, and chickens. Animal rescues often specialize in helping a specific type of animal—or even a specific breed—which makes it easy to find exactly the kind of pet you're looking for.

Your family will pay an adoption fee to cover things like vaccinations, microchipping, and spaying or neutering (important procedures that keep pets from having babies or developing certain illnesses).

Can't adopt a pet but still want to help animals? Check out page 84 for some volunteer ideas.

DAISY

TOMMY

COOKIE

Breeders

Some families buy animals from breeders if they need a specific kind of pet and can't find one at a shelter or rescue. You might go to a breeder if you need a pet that doesn't aggravate your allergies, or one that has the right qualities to become a service animal.

Always visit the breeder first to make sure the animals live in a healthy and happy environment. A good breeder will let you meet the animal's parents, give you a tour of the facility, and be very knowledgeable about the pets they raise. Keep in mind that animals from breeders are much more expensive than pets from shelters and rescues.

Pet stores

For the most part, you should only visit pet stores to buy supplies, or to adopt animals on special adoption days. Animals for sale at pet stores might come from breeders who keep animals in unhealthy, cramped conditions to make as much money as possible. Buying from a pet store could help keep those bad breeders in business.

If your heart is set on a small pet, like a fish, and you can't find one at a shelter, try finding a store that specializes in that animal. Someone at the store should be able to tell you where the animal came from and how it was raised.

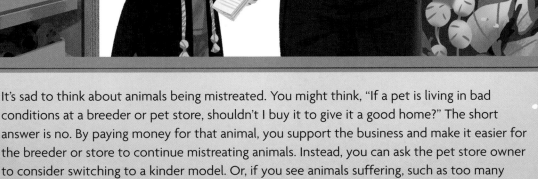

It's sad to think about animals being mistreated. You might think, "If a pet is living in bad conditions at a breeder or pet store, shouldn't I buy it to give it a good home?" The short answer is no. By paying money for that animal, you support the business and make it easier for the breeder or store to continue mistreating animals. Instead, you can ask the pet store owner to consider switching to a kinder model. Or, if you see animals suffering, such as too many cockatiels crammed into one cage, you can contact your local humane society for help.

Gathering Supplies

Before your pet arrives, make sure you have everything you need to make it healthy, happy, and comfortable in its new home. Here are some examples of different pets' basic needs:

Brushes come in many types. Read the label to make sure you get the right one for your dog's coat.

DOGS

Dog care book

Doggie Dos & Don'ts

Hygiene supplies

Flea, tick, and heartworm prevention

Treats

Collar (without prongs) or harness, ID tag, and leash (not retractable)

Toys

Poop bags

Bowls

Dog bed

Crate

Food (specific to your type of dog)

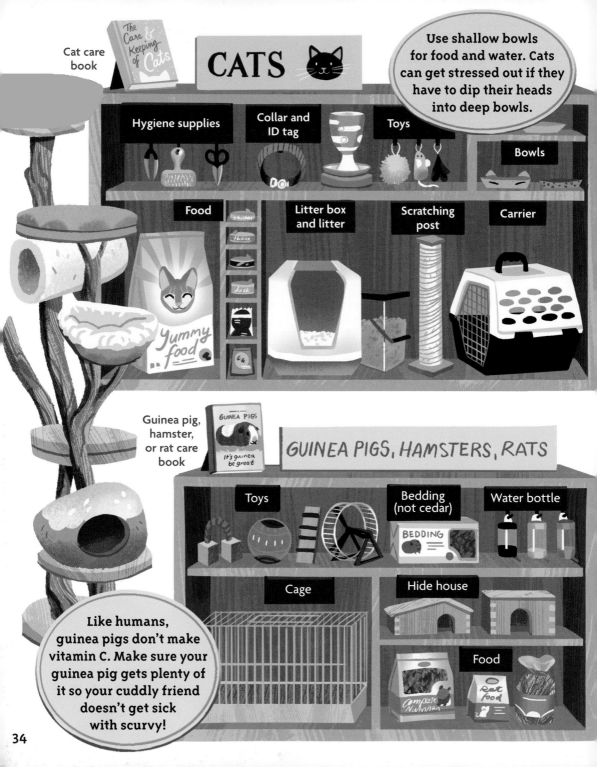

To help your bird get enough exercise, hide foraging bowls with food throughout its cage.

BIRDS

Bird care book

Dishes

Toys

Food

BIRDSEED

BiRD Pellets

Cage and cage liners

Rabbit care book

Healthy Habits for Rabbits

Rabbits

Rabbits' teeth never stop growing! Chew toys help keep their teeth short and healthy.

Toys

Nail trimmer

Water bottle

Food

Crate

Litter box and litter

Pen

Litter

Hay

35

A Healthy Habitat

Chances are, you live in a home designed for humans—it stays a comfortable temperature and has plenty of air for you to breathe. Dogs and cats can live happily in a home like that. But exotic animals, like snakes, lizards, and fish, need a different kind of habitat—one that mimics their home in the wild. It's your job to research exactly what environment your pet needs to stay healthy.

Fish and other underwater pets can't live in water straight from the faucet. Before you bring fish home, add conditioner to the aquarium, and use a test kit to make sure the water is perfectly balanced. A heater and thermometer help you make sure the habitat is a healthy temperature, and a filter is important for keeping the tank fresh between weekly cleanings.

Do careful research before adding a new species to your aquarium. Not all fish get along with each other, and some need very different types of water. For beginners, fresh-water fish are a great choice, because they can handle small changes in their water more easily than saltwater fish can.

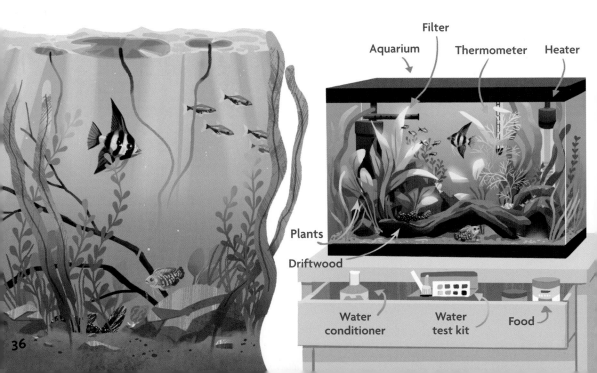

Filter
Aquarium
Thermometer
Heater
Plants
Driftwood
Water conditioner
Water test kit
Food

As a human, your body stays the same temperature inside, whether you're sledding down a snowy hill or sweating on the beach. But for reptiles and amphibians, their bodies change temperature when the environment around them does. Snakes, lizards, frogs, and turtles need a warming pad, heat lamp, and thermometer to keep the environment comfortable.

Plastic vivarium (with a lid)

Full-spectrum fluorescent light, on a timer

Two thermometers, for the cool and warm sides

Hiding places

Corn snake

Remember that if your pet eats live food, like mice or crickets, you'll need to provide a separate habitat for them, too!

Water dish

Under-tank heaters

Preparing Your Home

A lot of common things around a house—like stairs, cleaning supplies, and electrical outlets—can be dangerous to animals. Here are some pet-proofing tasks to check off before you bring your new pet home.

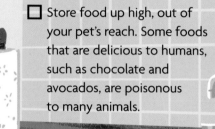

☐ Write down important phone numbers and post them on the fridge. Be sure to include numbers for your veterinarian, the emergency pet clinic, and the National Animal Poison Control Center.

☐ Store food up high, out of your pet's reach. Some foods that are delicious to humans, such as chocolate and avocados, are poisonous to many animals.

☐ Put latches on cupboards that hold cleaning supplies or medicine. Curious pets might put those things in their mouths, even if they taste terrible.

☐ Cover all garbage cans. Your pet might mistake them for fun, smelly caves to explore.

☐ Stock up on paper towels, pet odor neutralizer, and pet stain remover (but keep them away from your pet). Your animal is going to make messes, but you'll be ready.

☐ Keep the toilet lid closed, and put a sign in the bathroom to remind everyone to do the same. You don't want your pet drinking from the toilet or, worse, falling in!

☐ Use a gate to block dangerous areas in your house, like the stairs.

☐ Hide breakable items and knick-knacks that your pet could choke on.

☐ Hide electrical cords under rugs or furniture, or put coverings on them. You can also spray cords with anti-chew spray. Chewed-up cords are dangerous for you *and* your pet.

TAKING CARE OF A PET

You finally brought home
your new pet. Now what?

THE NAME GAME

One of the funnest things about getting a pet is choosing a name.
Here are some ideas to help you find the perfect one!

1. Fill in the blanks in each of these categories with your own ideas.

2. Circle your favorite name in each category. Get your family's input, too!

3. Call out each name. Which one does your pet respond to? Choose the name that makes her turn her head, perk up her ears, or run in your direction. (Or, if she doesn't have an opinion, ask your family to vote.)

> Animals respond best to names with one or two syllables. It's fine to choose a longer name—just come up with a short nickname to use for commands.

Your pet's favorite food

Steak

Zucchini

Crickets

Mouse

Ham

Sweet Potato

Tuna

Papaya

_____

_____

Your favorite food

Pancakes

Kimchi

Taco

Toast

Dumpling

Pizza

Curry

Sushi

_____

_____

Old-timey names

Genevieve

Walter

Mildred

Alonzo

Gertrude

Cornelius

Lucretia

Herschel

_____

_____

Punny names

Queen Elizardbeth (for a lizard)

Jennifurr (for a furry pet)

Emily Lickenson (for a pet that uses its tongue)

Finley (for a fish)

Droolius Caesar (for a dog)

Hermioneigh (for a horse)

Hamlet (for a hamster or pig)

Picatso (for a cat)

_____

_____

Names that *don't* describe your pet

Elephant (for a small pet)

Tiny (for a big pet)

Fluffy (for a spiky pet)

Gabby (for a silent pet)

Frisky (for a lazy pet)

Spots (for a solid-colored pet)

Zoom (for a slow-moving pet)

Shark (for any pet except a shark)

_____

_____

Names that describe your pet

Tank (for a big pet)

Nugget (for a small pet)

Vacuum (for a pet that eats a lot)

Ghost (for a white pet)

Butter (for a yellow pet)

Ash (for a black or gray pet)

Thunder (for a loud pet)

Secret (for a quiet pet)

_____

_____

Just-for-fun names

Tango

Flip

Kevin

Doodle

Sparkletoes

Trombone

Hopscotch

Grandma

_____

_____

Bringing Your Pet Home

Have you ever spent the night at a new friend's house? Maybe her parents served food you weren't used to, or something creaked in the attic, or you couldn't find the bathroom light in the middle of the night. Your new pet is having those same scared feelings!

To help your pet get used to her new home, take everything slowwwwwwwly. Introduce her to family members one at a time. Let each person cuddle her for a minute or two, and then take a break.

Don't be worried if your animal hides or doesn't want you to pet her. Squat down on her level, hold out your hand with your fingers pointing down, and wait for her to come to you. Say her name in a calm, quiet voice so she can get used to what you sound like. Coaxing her with a treat doesn't hurt either! If she still doesn't come, wait and try again later. She'll let you know when she's ready.

TREATS

Chow Time

It's up to you to make sure your pet eats a healthy diet and drinks enough water. Before you bring your pet home, ask what kind of food she needs, and how much. And keep in mind that her food needs might change as she grows older.

Since Clawdia is an adult, she needs two servings of dry food, once in the morning and once at night. Keep her water bowl full and fresh.

ADOPT MAXI

Mealtime is a lot of fun for both you and your pet. But feeding your pet too much or giving her the wrong kind of food can lead to low energy, an upset tummy, arthritis, or breathing problems. Here are some tips to keep your pet happy and healthy:

- Don't feed her scraps from the table.

- Keep human food out of reach.

- If your pet stops eating or drinking, or her weight changes in an unexpected way, call your vet.

- Use treats only for training, not for snacks.

- Learn which foods are dangerous for your pet, and keep those items out of reach. For example, grapes, sugar-free gum, avocados, and chocolate, can be deadly for dogs.

Keeping Track of Your Pet

No one wants to imagine their beloved animal running away or getting lost. But it happens. In fact, about one in every three pets will get lost at some point in its life.

Here are some ways to make it easier to reunite with your pet:

Make sure your pet always wears an **ID tag.** Include your name, address, and phone number on the tag. If someone finds your pet, they can contact you.

Register your pet. Most cities require registration to make sure certain pets—usually dogs and cats—have their required vaccines. And if your pet ends up at an animal shelter, having a registration helps the shelter get in contact with you.

Microchip your pet. A microchip is a tiny device that a veterinarian places under your pet's skin. If your pet's ID tag falls off, a veterinarian or animal shelter worker can use a scanner to find your information. Just make sure to register the microchip online and keep your information up to date.

These guidelines vary for different pets. Your goldfish will probably never run away, so he doesn't need a tag, registration, or microchip. A parrot, on the other hand, might need a microchip in case she flies out an open window. Ask a parent to help you research the rules in your town, and reach out to your vet if you need advice.

Speak Your Pet's Language

What is your pet trying to tell you? Match each animal's action to its meaning.

If you see this:

1. Your hamster is lying quiet and still, even though you're trying to play.

2. Your cockatiel is tapping her foot.

3. Your iguana is bobbing her head up and down while she's nice and relaxed.

4. Your cat is gazing at you, blinking verrrrrry slowly.

5. Your bunny is running around and around in circles.

6. Your dog is growling, with his ears flat against his head.

It might mean this:

A. "I want to play! Play with me! PLAY WITH ME!"

B. "I'm angry, and I might lash out. Back away slowly."

C. "You make me feel safe and content. This is my way of giving you a kiss. You're my very favorite kid."

D. "I'm so afraid. I can't run away, so I'm doing the only thing I can think of."

E. "This is MY space, and you can only come in here if I say it's OK. Mine!"

F. "Hey, thanks for the food! You're pretty cool."

Answers: 1. D; 2. E; 3. F; 4. C; 5. A; 6. B

TRUE Pet Story

Leila the Pet Vet

Nine-year-old Leila W. dreams of becoming a veterinarian one day, and she's starting her training now.

Leila's family fosters kittens until they're big enough to be adopted into forever homes. Leila helps with feeding the kittens, giving them medicine, and teaching them to feel safe around humans.

"I love spending time with the kittens, finding their personalities, and bonding with them," she says. Sometimes Leila bonds so deeply with a kitten that *her* house becomes the forever home.

Leila's impact on animals goes beyond the walls of her house. With her mom's help, she creates videos and social media posts under the name Leila the Pet Vet. She shares animal facts and pet care tips, encourages people to support animal shelters, and raises money for pets in need. She even created a coloring book to help support her local humane society.

When she was very young, Leila loved watching TV shows about animals. She thought working with animals for her career would be fun, so she visited the Texas A&M veterinary school to meet some real veterinarians. She even got to practice her pet surgery skills on a stuffed animal! Now she's sure that becoming a veterinarian is right for her. ♥

Grooming

Grooming doesn't just keep pets looking beautiful—it's essential to their health! Built-up dirt and oils can irritate animals' skin and make them sick. And grooming is a great time to notice suspicious bumps or sores that might need attention.

Each type of pet needs something different.

Dogs need to be brushed, trimmed (if they have long hair), bathed, and have their nails clipped.

Cats need to be brushed and have their nails clipped, but they almost never need baths.

Snakes can groom themselves as long as they have items in their tanks to rub against.

Most **birds** need a bath every week.

Fish don't need grooming at all.

Do research with your parents about what your pet needs, and talk to your veterinarian if you have questions.

The most common grooming task is brushing. Here's how to do it:

1. Get comfy. Sit on the floor and hold your pet in your lap.

2. Using a brush made for your type of animal, brush from the fur's roots to the tips. Brush in the same direction that the fur grows.

3. If you find a knot, gently untangle it.

4. When you're done, reward your pet with lots of cuddles!

Poop

Yep, your pet is going poop. *A lot*. It's your job to make sure she does it in the right place and to know how to clean it up.

Sometimes she'll make mistakes, especially while she's learning. (That's why you stocked up on stain and odor remover on page 38!) Never punish your pet for an accident, though. Just clean up the mess and help her do better next time.

Pets that go outside

Take your dog (or house pig!) outside often—about every hour for the first few days, or even more for small dogs. Stick to a regular schedule, and always let her out after she eats, wakes up, or has just finished playing. Use a command like "Go potty" so she understands what she needs to do. After she goes, give her a treat and tell her she's a good girl, and then spend some time playing outside. She'll be excited to go potty next time!

Always pick up your pet's poop, especially when you're out for a walk. Doing so keeps your neighborhood (and everyone's shoes) clean.

How to pick up poop

1. Put your hand in a poop bag, like you're wearing a glove.

2. Pick up the poop. It should never touch your skin.

3. Turn the bag inside out and tie a knot.

4. Throw the bag away in an outdoor trash can.

5. When you get home, wash your hands.

Pets that use a litter box

As soon as you bring your cat, rabbit, or ferret home, show her where the litter box is. Quiet corners that your pet can get to easily are the best places for a litter box. A cat might start doing her business there right away, on instinct. Rabbits and ferrets usually take a little more training. You can help them catch on by carrying them to the litter box after meals or when they act like they have to go. Reward them with a treat when they do a good job!

Remember to clean out the litter box every day. If it's dirty, your pet might not want to use it.

Pets that go in their cage

Some birds, guinea pigs, hamsters, chinchillas, and other furry animals can learn to do their business in a certain area of their cage, but it takes a lot of training and patience. If you're up for the challenge, ask your parents to help you research potty-training tips specific to your animal. Either way, clean the cage at least once a week.

Pets that live in a terrarium or aquarium

Don't even bother trying to tell a reptile, amphibian, or fish where to poop. Just be sure to clean the habitat once a week to keep it fresh.

Pet Peeves

What if your precious pet becomes your pet peeve?
Check out this advice from real girls.

My best friend's cat nibbles on people's toes at night while they're sleeping. To avoid it when I sleep over, I keep my toes under the blanket, or I ask my friend to put her cat downstairs for the night.

My friend's dog used to jump on me every time I walked in the door. Now I put my hand in front of his nose. It keeps him from jumping.

My bird used to wake me up very early in the morning with her loud tweeting. To prevent this, I put a dark sheet over her cage. Now she doesn't start singing until I take the sheet off.

To stop hamster wheels from squeaking, put a little cooking oil on the noisy part. Don't use regular oil, in case the hamster licks it. It really works!

I have two dogs. One of them always whined at the door when she wanted to go out. It drove us crazy! We filled a container with seeds and hung it from a string on the doorknob. Now both dogs just bang the container when they want to go out. It sounds like maracas and it's better than listening to whining!

If your pets bug you, maybe you don't spend enough time with them! Spend an hour just with your pets, walking and playing. Do something fun with them. You'll be closer to your pets, and your parents will appreciate it, too!

If you have a pet that acts up, it might be sick. My rabbit Klondike smelled bad, drank water all night, and kicked her bedding everywhere. I thought it was just a habit, but it turned out that she did it because she had an ear infection. Take the time to figure it out—don't assume it's just a bad habit.

Basic Training

Before learning fun tricks, your pet needs to master the basic rules of your home. She shouldn't jump on people, scratch them, or bite them. She's not allowed to leap onto the countertops or use the couch as a scratching post. What other rules does your pet need to follow?

Encourage your pet by giving her a treat when she behaves well. If she does something that's not OK, say, "Leave it!" and move her away from the tempting behavior. For example, if your dog chews up your refrigerator magnets, move her out of the kitchen and give her a chew toy to gnaw on instead.

When your pet misbehaves, don't pet her for a while. If you do, she might think you like how she's acting. Never, ever discipline animals by hurting or yelling at them. That just scares them. Pets don't understand the words we say, and it takes them a while to realize that "no" means you want them to stop. Be patient and consistent.

Teaching New Pets New Tricks

After your pet has mastered the basics, she might be ready to learn some new skills! Use treats, cuddles, and positive words to help her learn these tricks.

Sit
Dogs, cats

Hold a treat above your pet's nose and slowly move it behind her head. As your pet sits, say, "Sit!" in a serious voice and offer her the treat. Practice the trick over and over.

Lie Down
Dogs

While your pet is sitting, say, "Down!" Hold a treat close to the ground so she sees what she's supposed to do. When she lowers all the way down, give her the treat.

Down!

Shake or High-Five
Dogs, cats

While your pet is sitting, hold a treat in your hand and say, "Shake" or "High five." Hold up your other hand until your pet taps it, and then give her the treat. If your pet walks toward you or touches your hand with her head, start over.

High five!

Spin in a circle
Guinea pigs, hamsters, mice, rats

Hold a treat in your hand above your pet and say, "Circle." Move the treat in a circle so that your pet follows it. Then give her the treat and pet her. Repeat a few times over the next few days. Your pet knows the trick when she can spin in a circle without the treat.

Hop up
Rabbits

Hold a treat on the couch, and make sure your bunny sees it. Say, "Hop up!" and pat the couch where you want her to jump. Even if she doesn't make it up, give her a treat so that she associates the couch with a treat. Next time, hold the treat a little farther back on the couch. Eventually, she'll hop up to reach it!

Step up
Birds

Hold out your finger (for a small bird) or your arm (for a large bird). In a firm voice say, "Up." Your bird should step onto you. Give her a seed treat as a reward. (If you're worried about bites, start by holding out a wooden dowel.)

Follow the Finger
Fish

Put your finger on the aquarium. Once your fish pays attention, reward her with a pellet of food. Then move the finger back and forth and reward your fish each time she follows. Eventually, your fish will follow your finger without a treat.

Staying Healthy

Just like people, animals need check-ups to make sure they stay well. Most pets need to visit the veterinarian at least once a year, but very young or old pets might need more frequent visits. Set up a schedule with your veterinarian and stick to it.

Most veterinarians know how to care for cats and dogs. But if you have an unusual pet, it's best to find a veterinarian with special knowledge of that animal.

You might also need to visit the veterinarian if your pet gets sick or hurt. Spend plenty of time with your pet so you notice when something's not right. Keep an eye out for:

• Changes in how your pet eats

• Red or cloudy eyes, or discharge

• Vomiting or diarrhea

• Sluggishness

• Unexplained weight loss or gain

• Trouble breathing

• Accidents in the house, if your pet is housetrained

• Lumps or sores

• Changes in appearance, like ratty feathers or fur falling out

LOVING YOUR PET

Let your love for pets—and all animals—shine!

Pet Playtime

Playing with your pet every day is essential to keeping her happy and healthy. Try out one of these fun games during your next playtime!

Hide and Seek
Dogs

Ask a parent to hold your dog's collar. Show your dog that you have a treat, and then go into another room. Find a good hiding place, and call out, "Come!" Have your parent let go of your dog's collar. If your dog can find you, hand over the treat!

Obstacle Course

Hamsters, rabbits, guinea pigs, mice, rats

Gather old cardboard boxes, paper towel tubes, empty tissue boxes, and paper cups. Arrange them into obstacles for your small furry pet to run through, jump over, crawl under, and explore! Make sure to keep an eye on your pet the entire time in case she gets stuck or scared.

Cat and Mouse

Cats

Spread out a blanket on the floor or bed, and hide one of your cat's toys underneath. Get your cat's attention, and then move the toy around like it's a mouse under the blanket. Watch your cat chase and pounce on it.

Cockatoo Peek-a-Boo
Birds

Ask a friend to hold up a large towel or blanket over a bed like a tent. Put your bird inside. Run to one side of the tent and say, "Peek-a-boo!" As your bird hops toward you, run around to the other side of the tent and say, "Peek-a-boo!" again. Keep it up until your bird gets tired. Both of you will get some great exercise!

Peek-a-boo!

73

Pet Treats

Treats are great for letting pets know that they've done a good job. To show your pet some extra-special love, try making treats yourself!

Yappy Yum-Yums
For dogs

You will need:

- An adult to help you
- 2 six-ounce jars beef-and-vegetable baby food (Make sure they're free of onion and garlic, which aren't good for dogs.)
- 1 cup wheat germ
- 2 cups nonfat dry milk

1. Preheat the oven to 350 degrees. Cover a baking sheet with parchment paper.

2. Measure all ingredients into a large bowl and mix together with a fork.

3. Drop by small spoonfuls onto the baking sheet and flatten slightly.

4. Ask an adult to help you bake the treats for 12 to 15 minutes, until they're slightly brown at the edges. Let cool.

5. Seal in a plastic zipper bag and store in the refrigerator up to one week.

Picture-Perfect Peppers

For rabbits and guinea pigs

Rabbits and guinea pigs need a main diet of fresh hay and pellets, but these veggie treats are yummy and healthy for your pet a few times a week. (And guess what—they're tasty and healthy for humans, too!)

You will need:

- An adult to help you
- 1 red bell pepper
- 1 large cucumber
- 1 small cookie cutter

1.  Wash the vegetables thoroughly.

2.  With an adult's help, slice the top off the bell pepper. Then slice the pepper into sections, using the pepper's creases as a guide. Remove the excess white portion from inside.

3.  Using a cookie cutter, cut out shapes from the bell pepper sections.

4.  With an adult's help, cut the cucumber into ½-inch slices.

5.  Using the same cookie cutter, cut out a shape from the middle of the cucumber slices. Remove the shapes.

6.  Place the bell pepper shapes into the cucumber slices. They're picture perfect!

Serve right away. (The scraps are yummy, too.)

Turn treat time into a game! Hide a treat somewhere in your pet's space that she doesn't go very often, and cheer her on as she searches for it.

Silhouette Snack Saver

Store your pet's snacks in style with this homemade treat jar.

You will need:

- An adult to help you
- A glass jar with a lid (old jam or pickle jars work great!)
- Newspaper to protect your work surface
- Craft glue
- A small, plastic animal figurine that is the same species as your pet. You can find these at a dollar store, or maybe even in a toy box at home.
- Nontoxic craft paint
- A foam paintbrush

1.

Wash out the jar and lid and let them dry completely. Cover your work surface with newspaper.

2.

Glue the animal figurine on top of the lid. Let dry.

3. Dip your brush in the paint and dab it evenly over the figurine and lid. Let dry.

4. Decorate the jar with paint, stickers, or both. You might paint a paw print, write your pet's name, or stick on shiny stickers.

5. Fill the jar with treats and screw the lid on tight. Your pet will know a treat is in store when you reach for the jar!

Pet Pics

Show off your pet's beauty and charm with a photo shoot. Grab your camera and follow these tips to capture picture-*purr*fect poses.

Keep It Sleek and Simple

A plain, clean background keeps the focus on your pet. Before you start, clear away clutter or put your animal somewhere without a lot of stuff around. Zooming in on your pet gets rid of most of the background, too.

Get Your Pet's Attention

Ask a friend or sibling to be your assistant. When you're ready to take a picture, ask her to squeak a toy above your head. Your pet will look toward the sound, and you'll get a cute expression in the photo. This trick usually works best the first or second time you try it. After that, your pet might get bored.

Change Your Perspective

Squat or lie down to put the camera lens at the same height as your pet's eyes or lower. Your pictures will look more dramatic, and your photos will capture more of your pet's personality.

Turn Off the Flash

Many pets get scared or annoyed when they see flashing lights, so set your flash to OFF. Make sure there's enough light by shooting outside or in a room with lots of windows.

Show Some Spirit

To capture your pet's personality, get a picture of her doing something she loves. That might be swimming, running, climbing—or even sleeping! Keep your camera handy so that you can get great photos when the time comes.

Pawfect Professions

Looking for a way to turn your love for pets into a career? Take this quiz to match your skills to the perfect animal job.

1. Your friend is upset, but she doesn't want to talk about why. How do you respond?

   a. Give her a big hug.

   b. Make her a card.

   c. Give her the secret friendship sign that means you're always there for her.

   d. Distract her with something unexpected, like a unique rock you found over the weekend.

2. Which outdoor weekend activity would you try?

   a. Cleaning up a river—you love to have fun while making the world a better place.

   b. Kayaking—it's a chance to get some sweet photos of birds flying over the water.

   c. An obstacle course—you love physical challenges.

   d. Spelunking—exploring caves sounds like a blast.

3. What would you display above your bed?

a. An inspirational quote about caring for others

b. A close-up portrait of an elephant

c. A list of rules for people to follow in your room

d. A painting of a rain forest

CRAFTING WEDNESDAY : TODAY...

4. Your favorite online videos . . .

a. show people making a difference in the world.

b. inspire you with new ideas for arts and crafts.

c. teach you new skills.

d. make you think and ask lots of questions.

5. Which contest would you enter?

a. An egg-and-spoon relay—you're great at working with others.

b. A beautiful pet contest—your cat is so photogenic!

c. The world's largest obstacle course—with some hard work, you could win!

d. A star constellation contest in your neighborhood—who can find Aquarius first?

6. On your birthday, you'd love to receive . . .

   a. donations to your local animal shelter.

   b. a new camera lens.

   c. a fancy leash for your pup.

   d. a book about the world's strangest animals.

7. Which animal do you like best?

b. Rainbow lorikeet—what a colorful bird.

c. Golden retriever—they're reliable and friendly.

a. All cats and dogs—doesn't matter what breed.

d. Gila monster—you'd love to see one in real life.

Answers

Mostly a's
Animal Shelter Worker

You have a huge heart, and you're happiest when you're doing good for the world. You have a knack for making people and animals feel calm and loved, and you never give up. You might make a great animal shelter worker, as long as you can resist taking home every animal yourself!

Mostly b's
Animal Photographer

You were born to create. You look at the world with an artistic eye, and you can capture a pet's unique personality with the snap of a camera. Consider putting your skills to work as an animal photographer! For pet photo tips that you can start practicing now, check out page 78.

Mostly c's
Service Animal Trainer

You're a hard worker, and you work well with rules. You get excited by a new challenge and aren't afraid to share your opinion. You're brave, you stand up for others, and your family sometimes calls you a dog whisperer. You might make a great service animal trainer!

Mostly d's
Exotic Animal Veterinarian

You're a problem solver who never gets tired of seeing new things. You love to explore, you're fascinated by science and the world around you, and you're quite precise. Your love of unusual animals might lead you to a career in veterinary medicine—specifically in caring for exotic pets.

Making a Difference

If you've already showered your own pet with love, you might be ready for the next step: becoming an animal changemaker. A changemaker is someone who makes a positive difference in the world. And there are lots of animals in the world—in your neighborhood, even—who could use your love. Here are some ways to help:

Volunteer at an animal shelter

Shelters need volunteers to help with everything from cuddling animals, to cleaning out cages, to raising money, to educating the public about spaying and neutering. Check with your local shelter to see what tasks you can help with based on your age and whether you'll have a parent with you.

Raise money

Choose an animal organization you care about. With a parent's help, organize a bake sale, craft bazaar, lemonade stand, car wash—you name it—to raise funds for the cause. Make sure to let your customers know their money will help animals, and tell them about the organization you've chosen.

Foster a pet

Sometimes animals need temporary homes outside of a shelter. For a few weeks or months, a foster family gives a pet a safe place to live while she grows bigger, gets healthier, or learns social skills. Eventually, a permanent family adopts her. Fostering is a big responsibility, and it's not right for every family. Talk to a parent and someone at your local shelter to find out if it's a good fit.

Educate people

If there's a cause that's close to your heart, tell people about it! Do you want to make sure people in your town spay or neuter their pets? Do you want to spread the news about pets in the local shelter who need homes? Make posters, do a presentation for your class, or simply talk to your friends and family.

What other ideas do you have for making a difference in a pet's life?

Animal Shelter Pet Beds

Many animal shelters need blanket beds for dogs, cats, and other critters to sleep on. You can have fun and do good at the same time by making some to donate! Check with your local shelter first to make sure it can accept homemade pet beds.

You will need:

- Fabric scissors
- Ruler
- Masking tape
- Two 24-inch squares of fleece fabric in different colors or patterns

1.

Lay the fabric squares on a clean surface, on top of each other. If the fabric has a pattern, make sure the patterned side faces out.

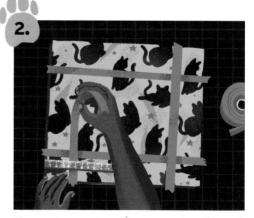

2.

Place a long strip of tape 4 inches from the edge of the fabric. This is your cut-to line. Repeat for each side of the fabric square.

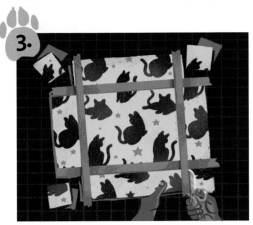

3. Following the masking tape, cut out a square from each corner of the blanket.

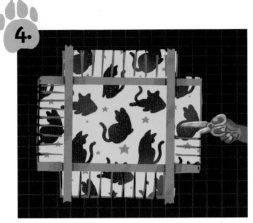

4. Make cuts from the fabric edge to the masking tape line, about 1 inch apart. Repeat all the way around the blanket.

5. Starting at one corner, tie two strips together, one from each piece of fabric. After you tie all the strips, peel off the masking tape.

6. Drop your blanket bed off at your local animal shelter to help a pet in need!

TRUE
Pet Story

Hiromi O.

Eleven-year-old Hiromi O. made a difference for dogs in her community. When she was in second grade, her class learned about the many stray dogs in their part of the Navajo Nation. The nearest animal shelter was three hours away, so the dogs had nowhere to go.

Hiromi felt bad for homeless dogs, even though she'd had a bad experience with one. Hiromi's dog Pepper was killed by a stray dog that was trying to bite her grandma. "The worst thing was, it was a dog that didn't have a home," Hiromi explained. "It was a dog that wasn't being taken care of."

If her town could build an animal shelter, Hiromi thought, more dogs would have a safe place to stay. She and other students wrote letters to community leaders explaining the issue and asking them to build a shelter. The leaders invited them to present their ideas at a community meeting.

Even if it takes many years to make the shelter a reality, Hiromi says educating people about the stray dog issue was important. She wants everyone to show all dogs the same kind of love she gives to her own pets. ♥

Eventually, all pets die. Saying goodbye is tough—maybe the hardest thing you've ever done.

Some pets pass away at home. Other pets become too old or sick to live comfortably, so a vet helps them die peacefully and without pain. This process is called *euthanasia*, though many people call it "putting a pet to sleep." No matter how a pet dies, losing one is sad. Really, really sad.

It's normal to feel upset, angry, lonely, and even guilty. Maybe you wish you could've done something to keep your pet alive. Or maybe you regret not spending more time with your pet when you had the chance. Whatever you're feeling, it's completely normal.

My dog died this month. My tummy hurts so bad. I hug my stuffed animal, but it's not the same.
Keisha

This feeling won't last forever. To help your tummy feel better, take a slow, deep breath. Count to four in your head while you breathe in through your nose. Let your belly swell out as you take in air. Then count to four again as you breathe out through your mouth. Do this several times. Ahhhhhh.

When you're ready, talk about your feelings with a parent or friend. Chances are, they're sad about your dog dying, too.

My cat just died. I'm almost happy because he was very old and in a lot of pain. I'm still sad, but deep inside I'm a little happy. Is this OK?
No more pain

Of course it's OK. Feelings of grief are complicated. You can be sad that your cat is gone and glad that his pain is over at the same time. Try making a collage of photos of your cat to display on your wall. Or fill up a journal with doodles and memories. After a while, your sadness will fade and you'll be left with happy memories of the good times you had together.

One of the best ways to start healing is to hold a ceremony for your pet. Here are some ideas to make the day special:

Make a scrapbook that shows the best moments from your pet's life.

Play a song that was special to you and your pet.

Prepare a treat inspired by your pet, like cupcakes with frosting paw prints.

Ask your friends and family to **stand in a circle.** One at a time, each person can share their favorite memory of your pet.

Write your pet's name on a small stone, and keep it on your desk as a keepsake.

With your parents' help, **plant a flower or tree** in memory of your pet.

In loving memory of Dexter

Some families bury their pet in a pet cemetery, or in a backyard. Others store their pet's ashes in a pretty container or scatter the ashes in a special place. Other families ask a vet or city official to take the pet's body away. It doesn't matter which method your family chooses—as long as you remember your pet with love, you're doing it right.

Eventually, the pain of losing your pet will go away. Someday you might even be ready to get a new pet. Your pet's memory will stay alive in your heart.

Love Pets, Always

Loving a pet is full of highs and lows, fun and frustration, and joy and sadness. Because you're an animal-lover, you cherish all of it.

I ♥ Boxers

Now that you have all these pet care skills under your belt, it's time to put them into practice each and every day. How will you show your love of animals?

Here are some other American Girl books you might like:

Write to Us!

Send your true pet stories to:

Pets Editor
American Girl
8400 Fairway Place
Middleton, WI 53562

All comments and suggestions received by American Girl may be used without compensation or acknowledgment. We're sorry—photos can't be returned.

Discover online games, quizzes, activities,
and more at **americangirl.com/play**